Above the Ashes

Above the Ashes by Casey Bunn
Copyright © 2024 by Casey Bunn

ISBN ebook 979-8-9904859-1-4
ISBN Paperback 979-8-9904859-0-7

Library of Congress Catalog Number:
2024907858

Illustrated by Elsa Linsky

Published by KWE Publishing, www.kwepub.com

Cover & interior design by Michelle Fairbanks, Fresh Design

First Edition. All rights reserved. No part of this publication may be reproduced in any manner whatsoever without written permission from the author, except in the case of brief quotations embodied in critical articles or review.

Above the Ashes

Written by Casey Bunn . Illustrated by Elsa Linsky
Dedication Page Illustration by Bridget George

This book is dedicated to my sweet husband and babies, to our family and friends who circled around us with strength and to the heroic Hanover firefighters who were there. You all were a part of the light in our darkness. Thank you sincerely.

Lieutenant James Reed

Lieutenant Spencer Ayers

Firefighter/Medic Bobby Visco

Firefighter/Medic Bobby Wellman

Firefighter/Medic Chris Coleman

Firefighter/Medic Todd Williams

Firefighter/Medic Pierce Echols

Firefighter/Medic Bo Young

Firefighter/Medic Kevin Herrity

Firefighter/Medic Caleb Allen

Captain
Cameron Bendall

Lieutenant
Brian Grimes

Lieutenant
Ryan Jordan

Firefighter/Medic
Bryan Dempsey

Firefighter/Medic
Will Green

Firefighter/Medic
April Thrift

Firefighter/Medic
Kip Berry

Firefighter/Medic
Justin Unger

Firefighter/Medic
Matt Micucci

Firefighter/Medic
Elly Cetin

Firefighter/Medic
David Pitts

I'm Jilly. I'm eleven years old, and I like gymnastics and horseback riding. We started a garden, and I got to pick what we planted. I also raised my chickens from babies and love taking care of them. My dog, Rosie, loves to fetch. She brings the toy back and bangs it on your leg so you will keep playing with her. Our family loves to spend time **together and** go on adventures.

I'm Charlie. I'm nine years old, and I like baseball and jiu-jitsu. My dog, Tush, is Rosie's brother and loves to be just where you are. He will not fetch anything, but he will let his sister get it, and he will stay right at your feet. My favorite thing to do is to build ramps out of things I find and ride over them with my bike or scooter. Then, I grab my sister and show her what I've made. Together, we jump and whiz around. Sometimes, we argue about who takes care of the chickens, but mostly, we just scout out our next adventure.

The day of the fire was a normal day. I had school and then riding lessons. Someday, I want to have a barn of my own because I love to spend time with the ponies. We left the house, and we kissed our dogs goodbye and each other goodbye. Then, I was off to riding class.

The day of the fire, we dropped Jilly off at the barn and headed to play some baseball with my team. I'm just learning to play, so practicing with my dad has been the best. I can tell I'm getting better. We play in the yard until it gets too dark to see the ball fly.

 I rode home from riding that day with my neighbor friend, Clara. At the driveway, my eyes were wide. The house was on fire—and not just a little bit. I first thought about my dogs. Mom was there, and then the fire trucks came. The firemen were very fast and worked hard to put the fire out.

I worried about my dogs and cats. They told me they went to sleep and woke up in heaven. Rosie would be surrounded by toys there, and Tush would get pets and have his belly rubbed nonstop.

There's only happy in heaven. It's better than anything we could have given them here, so I'm happy to know they are safe after all.

That night, we stayed at our neighbor's house. They have four girls about our ages, and the ten of us, plus my mimi and bobo, were very cozy. Our pastor brought us each a bag with some PJs and other clothes, shoes, and toothbrushes. It was a little like Christmas morning. We were surprised by our bags, and we smiled as we looked through them.

In the morning, our teacher, Holly, came over and we did school while Mom and Dad planned. The main thing was that our family was safe. My mom said, "Praise You, Jesus. Praise You, Father. Glory to God." It really is amazing. We lost everything, but we know we are loved, and we can hold onto that.

Dad told me that we have each other and that things would be okay.
But the next morning, things didn't feel okay. I wasn't sure
where we would live, and it felt strange to have nothing
and wonder how things would be. I felt scared.

But when we made pancakes in aprons and hats, I was happier.
We got to live with the Maddens until we found our camper, and it was like a
sleepover with friends every night. Mom said life was precious and that we
needed to be thankful for every day we have together.

To be honest, things that were a big deal before just suddenly got not
so big. My mind changed really fast. Now, I'm just glad we are here.

 My uncle and auntie helped collect clothes and things people wanted to share with us. So many people came by that their doorbell broke! We had to try on a lot of clothes and shoes, which was not my favorite, but I am happy so many people were kind.

When we say people are kind, we mean really kind—even ones who didn't know us. Our BB and grandpa surprised us big time. Strangers brought gift cards, Bibles, clothes, toys, bags, and books. Some things were funny, and we laughed a little, which felt good. We got a doll that looked just like a close friend, except with very messy hair, dressed up as a flight attendant. Dad danced her around and sang.

It took a few months for me to be able to realize this, but
God turned the fire into a blessing. Why?
Because He's gonna give us a new house,
He's gonna give us new dogs, and He's gonna give us new
everything. Plus, we have seen miracles,
and we can tell people about that too.
We are supposed to be a light for others and use
this story to bring hope to others who need it.

When we see photos of the fire or talk about it, sometimes it feels like it's happening now. Mom said not to feel anxious or fearful and that God says we can capture our thoughts to pass them to Christ.

I was confused about what that meant, so she said to imagine my scared feelings being packaged up in a little ball and tossed right over to Jesus to handle. It really does make me feel better to see that in my mind.

You can also just imagine those feelings piled on a plate in front of you at a table—worry, fear, anger, sadness. In my mind, I push them across the table with my hands to Jesus, who sits on the other side, ready to receive all my icky stuff.

He handles it better than me, so Mom says to pass it over and ask Him to fill the hole where those thoughts sat with peace, protection, and love. We are not designed to carry troubles on our own, but God can carry those feelings for us.

*The Lord is close to the brokenhearted;
he rescues those whose spirits are crushed.
Psalm 34:18*

It's okay to be sad and scared, but not forever. That's normal, but Jesus does not want that for our lives for a long time. So what do we do when we're sad or scared? Ah-ha! We capture that thought, ball it up, and pass it over. Take it in our mind and throw it away from us off to heaven.

We can also write scripture that speaks the truth about what has happened. We can feel better and post them up in our space. We can talk about what we are feeling and not be scared to say what we think. We can ask for snuggles and prayers, and we can be honest about our thoughts.

Psalm 16:2
"I say to the Lord, 'You are my Lord; apart from you I have no good thing.'"

Psalm 16:5
"Lord you alone are my portion and my cup; you make my lot secure."

Psalm 34:4
"I sought the Lord and he answered me, he delivered me from all my fears."

Isaiah 41:13
"For I am the Lord, your God, who takes hold of your right hand and says to you, do not fear I will help you."

Matthew 6:34
"Therefore do not worry about tomorrow, for tomorrow will worry about itself. Each day has enough trouble of its own."

Isaiah 6:3
"Holy, holy, holy is the Lord Almighty; the whole earth is full of his glory."

Joshua 1:9
"Have I not commanded you? Be strong and courageous. Do not be afraid; do not be discouraged, for the LORD your God will be with you wherever you go."

Rev 4:11
"Worthy are you, our Lord and God, to receive glory and honor and power, for you created all things, and by your will they existed and were created."

Jeremiah 29:11
"'For I know the plans I have for you,' declares the Lord,'plans to prosper you and not to harm you, plans to give you hope and a future."

This is not a curse, and we did nothing wrong to deserve it. I know God has a perfect plan, and good will come from bad as long as we believe and trust in Him.

*And we know that in all things God works
for the good of those who love him,
who have been called according to his purpose.
Romans 8:28*

When we went looking for a camper to stay in, it was awfully fun to slip into the bunks in all the different kinds. There were lots of options, and the camper we chose had a bed that moved up and down so a table could fold underneath. It was going to be our next adventure.

Jesus wants you to know that in your time of sadness, He is right next to you. The devil wants you to stay sad, take away your hope, and fill you with fear.

But you are protected and loved, and you can say,
"Go away, devil, in the name of Jesus," and he will; he has to.

Angel blast that devil away!
Imagine light all around you, glowing outward.
You have a superpower, and His name is Jesus.

Do not fear for I am with you;
do not be dismayed for I am your God.
Isaiah 41:10

I'll tell you about a miracle. When our house was gone,
they came to take all the ash and mess away and flattened the ground. Some
weeds sprung up right where the fire started.

Except, they weren't the weeds we thought they were.
They were sunflowers. A small family of them, just our sizes—
a daddy and mommy sunflower and two little ones.

My mom and mimi love sunflowers. They grow nowhere else on our land. They stayed alive while the land was cleared, uncrushed. In all the earth, sunflowers grew up there to show us that He had things under control.

*Glory belongs to God, whose power is at work in us.
By this power he can do infinitely more than we can ask or imagine.
Ephesians 3:20*

We also rescued a family of four kittens. I told my mom
that God gave me a vision of us snuggling these kittens,
and I saw us smiling with them. They needed a home just like us.
They bring us plenty of joy. They live outside in a cat house next to
our chickens. I'm happy God gave us these
new family members while we wait on our new house.

The gift of realizing what matters most in life was given to my brother and me early. The best advice I have is this—care about God most because everything else falls in place when you do that. Thank you for letting us share our story and share our hope.

FOR PARENTS

God forbid this happen to you,
you do not have time for anything. Please get out.

Fire comes like a thief. If you are like me in the past, you've thought of things you'd try to grab if your home was on fire (but your family was safe) and if "you had a few minutes to grab things." You don't. It's not like a campfire you are begging to get big; it literally consumes. It took one minute to go from one room to the whole house. Please make a family plan.

We are most thankful for what we have seen God do in others and in us during this tragedy. He

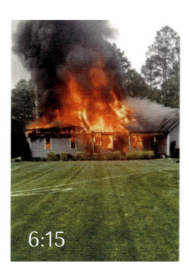

gets the glory, and our biggest hope is that blessing is poured into your life because of this too.

I was just so thankful we were together and thankful to God for His goodness in providing that. Every night for years, we have said a prayer, and we have always asked God to use us to be a light for Him. **This is His moment.**

Jilly's horse trainer said to me two days after our fire, "The devil doesn't get to steal from the daughter of a King and get away with it."

Isn't that the truth? That's the truth for you too in whatever's been stolen from you, so claim it, my brothers and sisters in Christ. We serve a big God, and He loves us.

I knew it would be hard, but we would be okay. I prayed God's glory shine through, that good things would pour out for us and for others. That is exactly what's happened. I know God has a strategy, and I couldn't have guessed this for our family, but I also know He will make good come from bad.

Check your smoke detectors and insurance limits, take a video of the rooms in your house so you can itemize your house easily, take pictures of things you cherish that are irreplaceable, get a safe for your important papers, take action on any lingering things you have been meaning to do, and don't wait for a tragedy to overcome family or friend tensions. Don't be fearful, but do be prepared.

Act now. Our pets and house disappeared in a minute.
Everything could change in an instant.

*Lift up your heads, O gates! And be lifted up,
O ancient doors, that the King of glory may come in.
Who is this King of glory? The Lord, strong and mighty,
the Lord, mighty in battle!*

Psalm 24:7-8

About the Author

CASEY BURKE BUNN is a first-time children's book author from Hanover, Virginia, who was inspired to share her family's story of overcoming tragedy after their home was destroyed by a fire in 2023. With faith and love from her community, Casey's family began to rebuild their lives. Casey created *Above the Ashes* to help readers like her own children who have experienced similar challenges know that they are not alone—and that life after a disaster can be beautiful and filled with hope. It's a perspective all people can benefit from, and she hopes this story brings light to the world.

To contact Casey, you can reach her at AboveTheAshesBook.com or LinkedIn. Special thanks to her company Handsocks for making this book possible.